ESSENCE, NOT EXCESS

Everything You Need, Nothing You Don't

"Simplicity is the ultimate sophistication."
– *Leonardo da Vinci*

by
Niroshi Lawinjeya

Copyright © 2025 by Niroshi Lawinjeya

All rights reserved. No part of this book may be reproduced, stored in a retrieval system, or transmitted in any form or by any means, electronic, mechanical, photocopying, recording, or otherwise, without prior written permission of the author, except for brief quotations used in reviews, articles, or critical analysis.

This book is a work of nonfiction. While every effort has been made to provide accurate and reliable information, the author makes no representations or warranties of any kind regarding the completeness, accuracy, or suitability of the content. The author and publisher disclaim any liability in connection with the use of this book.

For permissions or inquiries, contact:

[niroshilawinjeya@gmail.com]

Table of Contents

Introduction 1

How to use this book 3

CHAPTER 1: Minimalist Mindset 4

CHAPTER 2: Home & Living Spaces 6

CHAPTER 3: Work & Productivity 15

CHAPTER 4: Health & Wellness 20

CHAPTER 5: Relationships & Social Life 25

CHAPTER 6: Money & Consumption 29

CHAPTER 7: Mind, Spirit & Self 32

CHAPTER 8: Environment & Sustainability 35

NOTE 38

Acknowledgement 39

About the Author 40

Introduction
****

Life can feel like an endless race, rushing between work, home, family, and the countless little tasks that fill each day. For me, the race became exhausting.

I am a mother, a woman, and a person who once believed I could do it all. But somewhere along the way, my days became crowded with too much to do, too much to own, and too little time for myself. My home felt overwhelming, my health was neglected, and I was constantly running yet never arriving anywhere that felt peaceful.

Then I discovered minimalism.

It wasn't about empty rooms or owning nothing. It was about learning to focus on what truly matters and letting go of what doesn't. It was about clearing my home, my mind, and my schedule so I could finally breathe.

Minimalism gave me more than space. It gave me clarity, motivation, and a sense of control over my life. It helped me find balance as a mother, as a woman, and as a human being.

This book is for anyone who feels overwhelmed, cluttered, or constantly behind. It is for those who want to slow down without falling behind. It is a guide you can read one page at a time, applying each idea directly to your own life.

Here, you will find both inspiration and practical tools. Each chapter will help you strip away the excess in your home, your work, your relationships, and your mind, so you can focus on the essence: what you truly need, value, and love.

Minimalism changed my life. I hope it will change yours, too.

How to use this book

This book is designed to be simple in both style and substance. You can read it cover to cover or jump straight to the area you most want to simplify.

Each chapter focuses on one area of life, from your home to your health to your relationships. You'll find:

- Short, clear guidance on applying minimalism to that topic.
- Interactive prompts (tick boxes, tables, or reflection questions) so you can take action as you read.
- *Minimalist Moments* lighthearted, relatable reminders that simplicity can also be fun.

Minimalism works best when you start small. Choose one action from a chapter, try it, and let the change settle before adding more. There's no rush; this is about building a lifestyle, not racing to a finish line.

CHAPTER 1

Minimalist Mindset

Minimalism is more than decluttering your shelves; it's about clearing space in your mind. This chapter will help you define what's truly important so you can focus your energy on what matters most.

Why Minimalism

Minimalism is a tool to clear the clutter—both physical and mental. When you own less, you gain space for the things that matter most.

Define Enough

Decide what "enough" means for you, not for the world. Stop chasing more when you already have what you need.

Focus

When you scatter your attention, nothing gets done. Choose one priority and give it your full energy.

Gratitude

The more you appreciate what you have, the less you crave

more. Gratitude shifts your focus from lack to abundance.

Declutter Guilt

Keeping something "just in case" is holding onto the past. Release it, and you release the weight it carries.

This chapter sets the tone and creates the mindset shift that makes all the practical steps possible. From here, we'll move into specific areas of life where you can put this mindset into action.

CHAPTER 2

Home & Living Spaces

Our homes should be places of rest, not stress. Yet clutter often creeps in quietly, one "just in case" item at a time.

This chapter will guide you through each room, helping your home feel open, functional, and peaceful.

Kitchen

You open the drawer, and it sticks. You tug, and a tangle of unused gadgets stares back at you. How many have you actually used this month? In the kitchen, clutter steals space, time, and even peace of mind.

Before you decide what to keep, ask yourself: Do I use it regularly? Does it add value or joy? Would I buy it again today? Do I already own something that does the same job? Most importantly, does it fit my current lifestyle? If the answer is no, let it go.

(Unless it's your coffee machine—no life without coffee, right?)

Essentials

- 1–2 good knives

- Cutting board
- 2–4 plates, bowls, and glasses per person
- 1 saucepan & 1 frying pan
- Mixing bowl
- Basic utensils
- Measuring set
- Daily-use appliance (kettle, coffee maker, etc.)
- A few storage containers

Excess

- Extra mugs or glasses
- Duplicate pans or gadgets
- Specialty tools rarely used
- Plastic containers without lids
- Chipped dishes or warped pans
- Unused appliances
- Expired pantry items

Minimalist Moment — The 3-Item Rule

If you could only keep three tools in your kitchen, which would they be?

Write them here:

1._____

2._____

3._____

Keep these in mind whenever you're tempted to add more.

Bathroom

A bathroom should feel fresh and functional, not like a storage closet. Yet bottles, half-used products, and old towels seem to multiply without notice.

Before deciding what to keep, ask yourself: Do I use this often? Does it serve a clear purpose? Would I buy it again today? Is it the best version I own? Does it make my space feel clean and calm? If it doesn't meet these standards, it's adding clutter, not value.

Essentials

- Daily toiletries you actually use
- 2–3 towels per person
- Hand soap and toothbrushes
- Basic cleaning supplies
- Small storage for personal items

Excess

- Expired products or makeup
- Duplicate shampoos or lotions
- Towels you never reach for
- Broken hair tools
- Samples you don't use

Minimalist Moment — One-Minute Declutter Challenge

Set a timer for one minute. Open your bathroom cabinet or drawer.

Remove at least three items you no longer use.

When the timer stops, put them straight in the bin or donation bag.

Living Room

The living room should be a place to relax—not where your eyes keep tripping over piles of magazines, tangled cables, and "decorative" items you don't even like.

Before keeping something, ask yourself: Does it make this space feel more comfortable or more crowded? Do I enjoy looking at it every day? Would I replace it if it broke? Does it reflect the life I want to live? If not, it's time to let it go.

(Yes, even if Aunt Margaret gave it to you in 1998.)

Essentials

- Comfortable seating
- Lighting you love
- A few decor pieces that bring joy
- Entertainment setup you actually use
- Small storage for remotes or books

Excess

- Stacks of old magazines
- Extra throw pillows you never use
- Knick-knacks with no meaning
- Furniture that blocks flow
- Unused electronics or cables

Minimalist Moment — One In, One Out Pledge

From today, every time you bring something new into your living room, remove one item you no longer need.

Write your pledge here:

"I promise to remove _____ every time I add _____."

Bedroom

Your bedroom should feel like a calm retreat, not a laundry room in disguise. Clutter here doesn't just crowd your space it can crowd your sleep.

Before you keep something, ask yourself: Does it help me rest or prepare for the day? Do I use it regularly? Would I buy it again today? Is it worth the space it takes up? If the answer is no, let it go.

(And yes, that chair covered in clothes counts as clutter even if you call it "the floordrobe.")

Essentials

- A comfortable bed with good linens
- Bedside table or shelf
- A lamp or soft lighting
- Clothing you actually wear
- One or two personal decor pieces

Excess

- Piles of unread books
- Clothes that don't fit or suit you
- Decorative pillows you remove every night
- Furniture you don't use
- Random storage boxes gathering dust

Minimalist Moment — The 3-Item Rule

If you could only keep three non-furniture items in your bedroom, what would they be?

Write them here:

1. _____

2. _____

3. _____

Kids' Room

A child's room should be a space for play and rest, not a museum of every toy, game, and piece of clothing they've ever owned. The truth is, kids often play with the same few favourites, while the rest becomes clutter.

Before keeping something, ask yourself: Does my child use or wear this often? Is it age-appropriate? Would I buy it again today? Is it in good condition? Does it support how they play or learn? If not, it's probably ready for a new home.

(And remember—your kid's "treasure" might just be a rock from the park. Keep the memory, not the rubble.)

Essentials

- Age-appropriate clothing they actually wear
- A small selection of favourite toys
- Books they enjoy reading or hearing
- Storage for toys and clothes
- Bed and bedding suited to their needs

Excess

- Broken or incomplete toys
- Outgrown clothes

- Games with missing pieces
- Duplicate stuffed animals
- Old school projects or art you don't intend to keep

Minimalist Moment — One-Minute Declutter Challenge

Set a timer for one minute. Have your child choose three toys or books they no longer use.

Donate them together—it teaches them generosity and creates space for what they love most.

Wardrobe

Clothes should make you feel confident and comfortable, not overwhelmed every time you open the closet. If you're struggling to choose what to wear, it might be because there's too much to choose from.

Before you keep something, ask yourself: Do I wear this often? Does it fit me well? Does it suit my current lifestyle? Would I buy it again today? If the answer is no, it's time to let it go.

(And yes, you're allowed to say goodbye to those "someday jeans"—they know you've moved on.)

Essentials

- Clothes you actually wear and love
- A few versatile shoes
- Seasonal outerwear
- Everyday accessories you use

- Quality over quantity

Excess

- Clothes that don't fit or flatter
- Shoes you never wear
- Trend pieces you bought on impulse
- Duplicate items in the same color/style
- Damaged clothing you don't repair

Minimalist Moment — Closet Countdown

Choose 10 items from your wardrobe that you haven't worn in the last year.

Place them in a box. If you don't reach for them in the next 30 days, donate them without opening the box again.

CHAPTER 3

Work & Productivity

Work should challenge and inspire you, not drain every ounce of your focus. Minimalism at work isn't about doing less; it's about removing what distracts you from doing your best. This chapter will help you simplify your workspace, your schedule, and even your digital life so you can focus on what truly matters.

Office / Workspace

Your workspace should help you focus, not remind you of everything you haven't done. A cluttered desk invites a cluttered mind—and that makes productivity harder than it needs to be.

Before keeping something on or around your desk, ask yourself: Does this help me work better? Do I use it regularly? Would I choose to set it up again if I started from scratch? Does it earn the space it takes up? If the answer is no, it's adding distraction, not value. (And yes, that dried-out pen collection counts as clutter.)

Essentials

- A clear desk surface
- A comfortable chair

- Computer or tools needed for your work
- A small set of stationery you actually use
- Task lighting
- One or two personal touches that inspire you

Excess

- Stacks of unprocessed papers
- Duplicate stationery or unused supplies
- Outdated tech or cables
- Knick-knacks with no meaning
- Open browser tabs you never use (digital clutter counts, too)

Minimalist Moment — The End of the Day

At the end of each workday, take two minutes to clear your desk. When you return, you'll start fresh instead of playing catch-up.

Time Management

Time is your most valuable resource but it's also the easiest to lose without realizing it. When you spread yourself too thin, even the most important tasks get buried under the urgent but unimportant.

Before saying yes to anything, ask yourself: Does this move me closer to my goals? Am I the best person to do this? Is it worth the time it will take away from something else?

(If your calendar is so full you have to schedule "breathe," it's time to rethink.)

Essentials

- A short list of daily priorities
- Clear boundaries for work hours
- Regular breaks to maintain focus and energy
- A calendar or planner that works for you
- Time blocked for deep work

Excess

- Back-to-back meetings without purpose
- Overcommitting to tasks or events
- Checking email every five minutes
- Multitasking that lowers quality
- Projects without clear deadlines

Minimalist Moment — The Rule of Three

Each morning, choose three main tasks to focus on. Get those done before anything else, and consider the day a success.

Meetings & Communication

Communication is essential—but constant communication kills productivity. Endless meetings, reply-all emails, and nonstop messages keep you busy without letting you get real work done.

Before scheduling a meeting, ask yourself: Can this be handled in an email? Does everyone invited need to be there? Is there a clear agenda and outcome?

(If the highlight of your meeting is free cookies, it's probably not worth having.)

Essentials

- Meetings with a clear purpose and agenda
- Short, focused communication channels
- Regular but not constant updates
- Respect for others' focus time
- Clear action steps after discussions

Excess

- Standing meetings with no clear need
- Reply-all email chains
- Vague or open-ended agendas
- Group chats with constant pings
- "Let's meet just to meet" culture

Minimalist Moment — The 15-Minute Meeting

Challenge yourself to finish your next meeting in 15 minutes or less. Shorter meetings force clarity and action.

Digital Minimalism

Your digital world can be just as cluttered as your physical one—

and it's harder to see. Overflowing inboxes, scattered files, and endless notifications quietly drain your focus.

Before keeping any app, file, or subscription, ask yourself: Do I use this regularly? Does it help me or distract me? Would I notice if it were gone?

(And no, you don't need seven weather apps.)

Essentials

- Organized folders for files
- A clear inbox with only current messages
- Tools that directly support your work
- Notifications only for important updates
- Regular backups for important data

Excess

- Apps you never open
- Outdated or duplicate files
- Email subscriptions you don't read
- Folders you can't even name
- Constant, unnecessary notifications

Minimalist Moment — The Digital Detox Hour

Pick one hour a week to close all tabs, mute notifications, and clear out digital clutter. Treat it like tidying your desk—but for your mind.

CHAPTER 4

Health & Wellness

Minimalism isn't only about the things we own—it's also about how we care for our bodies and minds. By taking a simpler, more intentional approach to health, we can

free ourselves from overwhelm, boost our energy, and create more space for the activities and people we truly enjoy.

Exercise

There was a time when exercise felt like just another chore squeezed into an already busy day. But when I let go of chasing "perfect" workouts and focused instead on movement I genuinely enjoyed, everything changed.

Minimalist exercise is about removing the pressure, the excess gear, and the guilt—and simply moving in ways that feel good for your body.

Movement Menu — Choose One Today

- ☐ 10-minute stretch
- ☐ A short walk outside

ESSENCE NOT EXCESS

- ☐ Dance to one song you love
- ☐ Bodyweight exercises (push-ups, squats, planks)
- ☐ Play a game with your kids or pet

(Because your body doesn't care if you worked out in fancy leggings— it just wants to move.)

I used to treat sleep as if it were optional—something I could trim whenever life got busy. But each time I did, I paid the price in grumpiness, brain fog, and a serious coffee dependency.

Minimalist sleep is about protecting rest like any other important appointment: keep your bedroom calm and clutter-free, avoid screens before bed, and give your body the chance to recharge fully.

Tonight, I will:

- ☐ Read a book before bed
- ☐ Dim the lights 30 minutes before sleeping
- ☐ Keep my phone out of the bedroom

(Because nothing says "I love myself" like not hitting snooze ten times.)

Stress

Stress thrives in chaos—in our schedules, our homes, and our minds. When I learned to quiet the noise and let go of the endless "shoulds," my shoulders finally dropped from around my ears.

Minimalist stress management isn't about avoiding life; it's about removing the unnecessary so your best energy goes to what truly matters.

This week, I will:

- ☐ Remove one commitment from my calendar
- ☐ Say "no" to something that doesn't serve me
- ☐ Take one 15-minute break just for me

(And yes, canceling plans to stay home in pajamas is a valid wellness strategy.)

Meals

There was a time when opening the fridge felt overwhelming—full of ingredients I had no idea how to use. Now, it's simple: only the foods I enjoy and actually eat.

Minimalist eating means fewer decisions, less waste, and more meals that genuinely make you feel good.

This month, I will:

- ☐ Write down five go-to meals I love
- ☐ Build my grocery list from those meals
- ☐ Clear out unused items from the fridge

(Bonus: you'll finally stop wondering what's growing in the back of the fridge.)

Ingredients

Open your pantry and you might spot five kinds of pasta, half a dozen oils, and spices you bought for that one recipe and never touched again. Time to simplify.

Minimalist ingredients focus on the foods you actually use — versatile staples you can turn into multiple meals without the waste.

Pantry Audit Table

Ingredient	Used Weekly	Rarely Used	Replace / Donate
	☐	☐	☐
	☐	☐	☐
	☐	☐	☐

(If it's expired, the decision's already made for you.)

Waste

Eating well isn't just about what you put in your body — it's also about what you don't throw away. Every bit of wasted food is wasted money, time, and resources.

Minimalist waste reduction starts with buying only what you need and making the most of what you already have.

Try this:

☐ Plan your meals before shopping

☐ Store food properly so it lasts longer

- ☐ Keep a "use me first" box in the fridge for items close to expiry

- ☐ Learn one or two "leftover rescue" recipes (And remember: the freezer is your friend.)

CHAPTER 5

Relationships & Social Life

Minimalism isn't just about what you own — it's also about the relationships you keep and the way you spend your social energy. By being intentional with your connections, you can create more space for the people and experiences that truly matter.

Friendships

There was a time I tried to keep in touch with everyone — school friends, old co-workers, even people I'd only met once at a party. But spreading my energy that thin meant my closest friendships weren't getting the attention they deserved.

Minimalist friendships focus on depth over breadth. It's not about how many people you know — it's about how many people truly know you.

Connection Audit Table — Friendships

Name	Energizing	Neutral	Draining	Action to Take
	☐	☐	☐	☐
	☐	☐	☐	☐
	☐	☐	☐	☐

(Because "liking" a post on social media doesn't count as catching up.)

Family

Family relationships can be both the most rewarding and the most complicated. Minimalism here means holding on to the traditions, habits, and time together that bring joy — and letting go of the ones that drain you.

Sometimes that looks like fewer big, stressful gatherings and more small, meaningful moments.

Connection Audit Table — Family

Name	Energizing	Neutral	Draining	Action to Take
	☐	☐	☐	☐
	☐	☐	☐	☐
	☐	☐	☐	☐

(Quality time beats quantity every time.)

Social Commitments

It's easy to say yes to every invitation — until your calendar starts to look like a game of Tetris. Minimalist socializing is about choosing events and activities that energize you, not ones that leave you drained.

Connection Audit Table — Social Commitments

Event / Activity	Energizing	Neutral	Draining	Action to Take
	☐	☐	☐	☐

| | ☐ | ☐ | ☐ | ☐ |
| | ☐ | ☐ | ☐ | ☐ |

(And remember — "Thanks for inviting me, but I can't make it" is a complete sentence.)

Community & Giving

Minimalism isn't about turning inward; it's about creating space to give outward. When you spend less time and energy on things that don't matter, you free yourself to share more with others.

This might look like volunteering, donating items you no longer use, or simply showing up for someone who needs you.

Connection Audit Table — Community & Giving

Person / Group	Energizing	Neutral	Draining	Action to Take
	☐	☐	☐	☐
	☐	☐	☐	☐
	☐	☐	☐	☐

(Because the most valuable thing you can give is your attention.)

CHAPTER 6

Money & Consumption

Minimalism doesn't just create space in your home — it also brings freedom to your finances. When you know where your money is going, you can stop spending on what doesn't matter and start directing it toward what truly does.

This chapter isn't about spreadsheets or strict rules. It's about clarity making sure every dollar you spend has a purpose and reflects your priorities. We'll explore how to budget simply, spend intentionally, avoid debt traps, and shop with more awareness.

Think of it as decluttering your bank account and your shopping habits. The result? Less stress, more freedom, and the ability to enjoy life without financial clutter.

Budgeting

Minimalist budgeting isn't about restriction — it's about clarity. Every dollar should have a purpose, whether it's covering essentials, creating joy, building savings, or giving generously.

Budget Priorities Table

Priority	Monthly Amount	Notes
	☐	☐
	☐	☐
	☐	☐

Spending Habits

Before buying, pause and ask:

- Do I need this?
- Will I still want it next week?
- Could I borrow it instead?

Impulse Buy Checkboxes

- ☐ Wait 24 hours before purchase
- ☐ Check if I already own something similar
- ☐ Decide if it supports my priorities

Debt

Focus on paying off the highest-interest debt first, then roll that payment to the next one.

Debt Snowball Tracker

Debt Name	Balance	Monthly Payment	Status
	☐	☐	
	☐	☐	
	☐	☐	

Conscious Consumption

Buy less, choose better, make it last.

CHAPTER 7

Mind, Spirit & Self

Minimalism isn't just about what's in your home or bank account — it's also about what's in your head and heart.

When your mind is cluttered with endless thoughts and your days are packed with no space to breathe, it's hard to fully enjoy life.

This chapter is about creating mental and emotional space. It's not about being silent or still all the time — it's about ensuring your inner world feels as calm and intentional as your outer one. We'll explore quiet time, hobbies, reflection, and growth — because the simplest life is one where peace begins within.

Quiet Time

When was the last time you sat in silence without reaching for your phone? Quiet time is where ideas grow and stress shrinks.

Mini Game — The 5-Minute Pause

- ☐ Find a comfortable seat
- ☐ Set a timer for 5 minutes
- ☐ Close your eyes and focus on your breathing

- [ ] If a thought pops up, notice it and let it pass like a cloud
- [ ] When the timer ends, write down one thing you noticed about how you feel

(Spoiler: you might like it enough to try for 10 minutes next time.)

Hobbies & Passions

Minimalism doesn't mean stripping away joy — it means creating more space for it. Your hobbies are the meaningful 'yes' in a sea of 'no.'

Passion Inventory Game

- Write down every hobby you've ever enjoyed
- Circle the ones you'd happily spend an afternoon doing now
- Pick one and make time for it this week
- Bonus: Let go of supplies or gear for hobbies you've outgrown

(Because you can't do everything — but you can do what lights you up.)

Self-Reflection

Life moves quickly — sometimes so quickly that we forget to pause and ask if we're still on the path we want. Self-reflection is that moment to stop, check the map, and make sure you're heading in the right direction.

3-Question Journal Prompt

1. What's working well in my life right now?
2. What's taking up space without adding value?
3. What's one small change I can make this week?

Personal Growth

Minimalism isn't about stopping — it's about making room to grow. When you clear away the noise and distractions, you create space to learn, explore, and become more of who you're meant to be.

Growth Challenge

- ☐ Learn one new skill this month (big or small)
- ☐ Read or listen to one inspiring book or podcast
- ☐ Try something that scares you — even just a little

(Because the best version of you doesn't come from having more — it comes from becoming more.)

CHAPTER 8

Environment & Sustainability

Minimalism and sustainability go hand in hand. When you live with less, you waste less. When you choose with care, you protect the planet. This chapter is about embracing simplicity in a way that also nurtures the world around you.

You don't have to transform everything overnight — small, intentional steps create lasting impact. The goal isn't perfection, but awareness and steady progress.

Energy & Water

Our homes consume more resources than we often realize. Minimalist living means using only what's truly necessary — and more often than not, that turns out to be less than we think.

Eco-Action Checklist

- ☐ Switch off lights when leaving a room
- ☐ Unplug devices not in use
- ☐ Take shorter showers
- ☐ Wash clothes in cold water when possible

- [ ] Use natural light during the day

(Your bills and the planet will both thank you.)

Transportation

Getting from point A to point B can be simpler, cheaper, and greener. Minimalist transport focuses on efficiency and impact.

Transport Swap Game

- For one week, swap one car trip for:
  - [ ] Walking
  - [ ] Cycling
  - [ ] Public transport
  - [ ] Carpooling
- Track how much time, money, or fuel you save (And yes, taking the scenic route on foot counts as "me time.")

Minimalist Shopping

Every purchase has a footprint. The most sustainable item is often the one you don't buy.

Buy or Pause?

- [ ] Can I borrow, rent, or find secondhand?
- [ ] Is it built to last?
- [ ] Will it replace something I already own?

(Impulse shopping is less tempting when you picture the landfill.)

Reducing Waste

Landfills are full of things that were once someone's "must-have." Minimalist waste reduction is about keeping items in use as long as possible and choosing reusable over disposable.

Waste-Less Challenge

- ☐ Bring your own bag and bottle
- ☐ Use reusable containers for lunch and storage
- ☐ Repair instead of replace
- ☐ Compost food scraps if possible

(I's amazing how small swaps can lead to big changes.)

NOTE

Minimalism isn't about owning nothing.

It's about owning, doing, and keeping only what truly matters.

You don't have to change your life overnight.

Start small—one drawer, one commitment, one thought.

Choose essence over excess, again and again.

The space you create—physically, mentally, and emotionally—becomes the place where clarity, joy, and freedom live.

Your life won't feel empty.

It will feel full of the right things.

Acknowledgement

To my family, for their patience, love, and constant reminders of what truly matters.

To my friends, who encouraged me when this book was just an idea.

To every reader who has chosen to explore a life of less — may you find more of what matters in return.

And to minimalism itself, for giving me clarity when I needed it most.

About the Author

Niroshi Lawinjeya was born in Sri Lanka and has lived in Germany and England. She is a web designer, a student, and a mother.

Her own journey into minimalism began as a way to declutter her space and mind. The transformation brought her clarity, spiritual connection, better decision-making, and unexpected health benefits.

Inspired by these changes, she wrote this book to help others experience the same freedom and focus that comes from living with essence, not excess.

Email: niroshilawinjeya@gmail.com

Essence, Not Excess

A Simple Guide to Living with What Truly Matters

In a world overflowing with possessions, commitments, and noise, minimalism isn't about owning less—it's about making space for what matters most.

In this clear, practical, and uplifting guide, Niroshi Lawinjeya walks you through every area of life—from your home and health to relationships, work, and even parenting—showing you how to release the excess and hold on to the essence.

Each page offers simple, focused guidance and gentle prompts to help you define what's essential in *your* life. No overwhelm, no rigid systems—just small, mindful steps toward a lighter, calmer, and more intentional way of living.

If you're ready to create room for clarity, connection, and joy,

this book will guide you there—one choice at a time.

"Clear the clutter, keep the clarity — discover the freedom of living with only what truly matters."